Traveler's Passport

America's National Parks

United States and Canada

Second Edition

©2016 Snipe International, LLC & Traveler's Passport
All rights reserved. No part of this book may be reproduced or utilized in any form or by any means, electronic or mechanical, including photocopy, recording, or by any information storage retrieval system, without permission in writing from the publisher.

How To Use Your Traveler's Passport

The *Passport to America's National Parks & The United States and Canada* has been designed to help you keep track of your visits to U.S. national parks, U.S. states, and Canadian provinces. Each national park is identified by its name, state, and date of foundation. Each U.S. state has a picture of its flag, a welcome sign, its capital, and state statistics. Each Canadian province or territory has a picture of its provincial flag, a welcome sign, a government building, and statistics. We have also included trivia for each state, province, or territory.

In the national park section, enter the park stamp under the photo in each entry. On each state, province, or territory page, enter the date of your visit in the box next to the state or province name. You can keep a visual record of your U.S. or Canada visits on the appropriate maps by highlighting the locations you have visited. The five U.S. regions are color-coded: **West (green)**, **Midwest (red)**, **Southwest (purple)**, **Southeast (orange)**, and **Northeast (blue)**. Each U.S. territory is represented by a modified purple rectangle; a red one represents each Canadian province or territory.

At the back of the Passport, there are American and Canadian trivia quizzes, as well as regional license plates to check off while you are traveling. Home schoolers, students, and teachers will find lesson plans and questions to extend their knowledge of American states and national parks in addition to Canadian provinces and territories at **www.snipe-international.com**.

My Passport Information

Your Picture Here

___
Name

___
Address

___
City

___
State / Province

___
Postal Code

___
Country

___
E-mail

___
Number of U.S. national parks and monuments visited

___
Number of U.S. states and territories visited

___
Number of Canadian provinces and territories visited

America's National Parks

The National Park Service was created by an act signed by President Woodrow Wilson on August 25, 1916.

Yellowstone National Park was established by an Act signed by President Ulysses S. Grant on March 1, 1872, the nation's first National Park.

The parks are listed alphabetically with their locations and dates founded. There is a place to have your Passport stamped at each National Park.

Acadia National Park	**Arches National Park**	**Badlands National Park**
		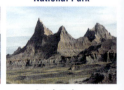
Maine July 8, 1916	Utah April 12, 1929	South Dakota November 10, 1978

Big Bend National Park

Texas
June 12, 1944

Biscayne National Park

Florida
June 28, 1980

Black Canyon of the Gunnison National Park

Colorado
October 21, 1999

Bryce Canyon National Park

Utah
February 25, 1928

Canyonlands National Park

Utah
September 12, 1964

Capitol Reef National Park

Utah
December 18, 1971

Carlsbad Caverns National Park

New Mexico
May 14, 1930

Channel Islands National Park

California
March 5, 1980

Congaree National Park

South Carolina
November 10, 2003

Crater Lake National Park

Oregon
May 22, 1902

Cuyahoga Valley National Park

Ohio
October 11, 2000

Death Valley National Park

California, Nevada
October 31, 1994

Denali
National Park & Preserve

Alaska
February 26, 1917

Dry Tortugas
National Park

Florida
January 4, 1935

Everglades
National Park

Florida
December 6, 1947

Gates of the Arctic
National Park & Preserve

Alaska
December 2, 1980

Glacier Bay
National Park & Preserve

Alaska
December 2, 1980

Glacier
National Park

Montana
May 11, 1910

Grand Canyon National Park

Arizona
February 26, 1919

Grand Teton National Park

Wyoming
February 26, 1929

Great Basin National Park

Nevada
October 27, 1986

Great Sand Dunes National Park & Preserve

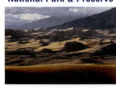

Colorado
September 13, 2004

Great Smoky Mountains National Park

North Carolina, Tennessee
June 15, 1934

Guadalupe Mountains National Park

Texas
September 30, 1972

Haleakalá National Park

Hawai'i
August 1, 1916

Hawai'i Volcanoes National Park

Hawai'i
August 1, 1916

Hot Springs National Park

Arkansas
March 4, 1921

Isle Royale National Park

Michigan
April 3, 1940

Joshua Tree National Park

California
October 31, 1994

Katmai National Park & Preserve

Alaska
December 2, 1980

Kenai Fjords National Park

Alaska
December 2, 1980

Kings Canyon National Park

California
March 4, 1940

Kobuk Valley National Park

Alaska
December 2, 1980

Lake Clark National Park & Preserve

Alaska
December 2, 1980

Lassen Volcanic National Park

California
August 9, 1916

Mammoth Cave National Park

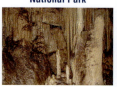

Kentucky
July 1, 1941

Mesa Verde National Park

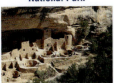

Colorado
June 29, 1906

Mount Rainier National Park

Washington
March 2, 1899

National Park of American Samoa

American Samoa
October 31, 1988

North Cascades National Park

Washington
October 2, 1968

Olympic National Park

Washington
June 29, 1938

Petrified Forest National Park

Arizona
December 9, 1962

Pinnacles National Park

California
January 10, 2013

Redwood National Park

California
October 2, 1968

Rocky Mountain National Park

Colorado
January 26, 1915

Saguaro National Park

Arizona
October 14, 1994

Sequoia National Park

California
September 25, 1890

Shenandoah National Park

Virginia
December 26, 1935

Theodore Roosevelt National Park

North Dakota
November 10, 1978

Virgin Islands National Park

U.S. Virgin Islands
August 2, 1956

Voyageurs National Park

Minnesota
April 8, 1975

Wind Cave National Park

South Dakota
January 9, 1903

Wrangell-St. Elias National Park & Preserve

Alaska
December 2, 1980

Yellowstone National Park

Wyoming, Montana, Idaho
March 1, 1872

Yosemite National Park

California
October 1, 1890

Zion National Park

Utah
November 19, 1919

America's National Monuments, Memorials, Preserves, & Recreation Areas

Cabrillo National Monument

California
October 14, 1913

Castle Clinton National Monument

New York
August 12, 1946

Golden Gate National Recreation Area

California
October 27, 1972

Jefferson National Expansion Memorial

Missouri
December 21, 1935

Mount Rushmore National Memorial

South Dakota
March 3, 1925

Mount St. Helens National Volcanic Monument

Washington
August 26, 1982

Oregon Caves National Monument & Preserve

Oregon
July 12, 1909

Statue of Liberty National Monument

New York
October 15, 1924

WWII Valor in the Pacific National Monument

Alaska, California, Hawai'i
December 5, 2008

United States of America

"In God We Trust"

Capital District: Washington, D.C.

Population: 311,591,917

Area: 3,794,083 sq. mi. (9,826,630 sq. km)

Language: English, Spanish

National Bird: Bald Eagle

National Flower: Rose

National Tree: Oak

States: 50

Territories: 5 (American Samoa, Guam, Northern Mariana Islands, Puerto Rico, & U.S. Virgin Islands)

"The Heart of Dixie" # Alabama

Capital:	Montgomery
Population:	4,802,740
Area (sq. mi.):	50,750
State Bird:	Yellowhammer
State Flower:	Camellia
State Tree:	Southern Pine
Economy:	Cattle, cotton, peanuts, dairy, watermelon

Date Visited:

Alabama workers built the first moon rocket.

"The Last Frontier" # Alaska

Capital:	Juneau
Population:	722,718
Area (sq. mi.):	570,374
State Bird:	Willow Ptarmigan
State Flower:	Forget-me-not
State Tree:	Sitka Spruce
Economy:	Dairy, cattle, hogs, barley, fish, crab, lumber

Date Visited:

Alaska was purchased from Russia in 1867 for $7,200,000, or two cents per acre.

Arizona   "The Grand Canyon State"

Date Visited:

Capital:	Phoenix
Population:	6,482,505
Area (sq. mi.):	113,642
State Bird:	Cactus Wren
State Flower:	Saguaro Cactus
State Tree:	Paloverde
Economy:	Cattle, lemons, pecans, watermelons, onions, lettuce

Arizona is the leading producer of copper in the U.S.A.

Arkansas   "The Natural State"

Date Visited:

Capital:	Little Rock
Population:	2,937,979
Area (sq. mi.):	52,075
State Bird:	Mockingbird
State Flower:	Apple Blossom
State Tree:	Pine Tree
Economy:	Rice, cattle, soybeans, cotton, eggs, turkeys, pecans

Sam Walton opened the first Wal-Mart store in Rogers.

"The Golden State"   California

Capital:	Sacramento
Population:	37,691,919
Area (sq. mi.):	155,973
State Bird:	California Quail
State Flower:	Golden Poppy
State Tree:	California Redwood
Economy:	Grapes, strawberries, almonds, oranges, cattle, dairy, dates

Date Visited:

One out of every eight U.S. residents lives in California.

"The Centennial State"   Colorado

Capital:	Denver
Population:	5,116,796
Area (sq. mi.):	103,729
State Bird:	Lark Bunting
State Flower:	R.M. Columbine
State Tree:	Blue Spruce
Economy:	Cattle, dairy, wheat, potatoes, eggs, sugar beets

Date Visited:

The world's first rodeo was held in Deer Trail on July 4th, 1869.

Connecticut — "The Constitution State"

Date Visited:

- Capital: Hartford
- Population: 3,580,709
- Area (sq. mi.): 4,845
- State Bird: Robin
- State Flower: Mountain Laurel
- State Tree: White Oak
- Economy: Dairy, aguaculture, corn, cattle, maple products

Connecticut was the first state to issue car license plates in 1937.

Delaware — "The First State"

Date Visited:

- Capital: Dover
- Population: 907,135
- Area (sq. mi.): 1,955
- State Bird: Blue Hen Chicken
- State Flower: Peach Blossom
- State Tree: American Holly
- Economy: Poultry, soybeans, potatoes, peas, cucumbers

Delaware was the first state to ratify the United States Constitution.

"The Sunshine State" — Florida

Capital:	Tallahassee
Population:	19,057,542
Area (sq. mi.):	53,997
State Bird:	Mockingbird
State Flower:	Orange Blossom
State Tree:	Cabbage Palmetto
Economy:	Oranges, sugar cane, cattle, dairy, peanuts, nursery

Date Visited:

St. Augustine is the oldest continuously-occupied European settlement in the U.S.A.

"The Peach State" — Georgia

Capital:	Atlanta
Population:	9,815,210
Area (sq. mi.):	57,919
State Bird:	Brown Thrasher
State Flower:	Cherokee Rose
State Tree:	Live Oak
Economy:	Poultry, cotton, eggs, peanuts, dairy, pecans, cattle

Date Visited:

Georgia is the leading producer of peanuts, peaches, and pecans in the U.S.A.

Hawai'i   "The Aloha State"

Date Visited:

Capital:	Honolulu
Population:	1,374,810
Area (sq. mi.):	6,423
State Bird:	Nene
State Flower:	Hibiscus
State Tree:	Kukui
Economy:	Pineapples, coffee, sugar cane, taro, papayas, macadamia nuts

Hawai'i is the only state that produces both coffee and pineapples.

Idaho   "The Gem State"

Date Visited:

Capital:	Boise
Population:	1,584,985
Area (sq. mi.):	82,751
State Bird:	Mountain Bluebird
State Flower:	Syringa
State Tree:	Western White Pine
Economy:	Dairy, cattle, potatoes, wheat, hay, sugar beats, apples

Idaho is the largest producer of potatoes in the U.S.A.

"The Prairie State" — Illinois

Capital:	Springfield
Population:	12,869,257
Area (sq. mi.):	55,593
State Bird:	Cardinal
State Flower:	Native Violet
State Tree:	White Oak
Economy:	Soybeans, hogs, eggs, corn, dairy, turkeys, cabbage

Date Visited:

The world's first skyscraper was built in Chicago in 1885.

"The Hoosier State" — Indiana

Capital:	Indianapolis
Population:	6,516,922
Area (sq. mi.):	35,870
State Bird:	Cardinal
State Flower:	Peony
State Tree:	Yellow Poplar
Economy:	Soybeans, hogs, hay, corn, tobacco, watermelon

Date Visited:

The Raggedy Ann doll was made in Indianapolis by Marcella Gruelle in 1914.

Iowa
"The Hawkeye State"

Date Visited:

Capital: Des Moines
Population: 3,062,309
Area (sq. mi.): 55,875
State Bird: Eastern Goldfinch
State Flower: Wild Rose
State Tree: Oak
Economy: Corn, hogs, honey, dairy, wheat, oats, apples

The world's largest cereal company, Quaker Oats, is located in Cedar Rapids.

Kansas
"The Sunflower State"

Date Visited:

Capital: Topeka
Population: 2,871,238
Area (sq. mi.): 55,875
State Bird: Western Meadowlark
State Flower: Sunflower
State Tree: Cottonwood
Economy: Wheat, cattle, soybeans, hogs, dairy, sorghum, pecans

The Pizza Hut restaurant chain was founded in Wichita.

"The Bluegrass State" — Kentucky

Capital:	Frankfort
Population:	4,369,356
Area (sq. mi.):	39,732
State Bird:	Cardinal
State Flower:	Goldenrod
State Tree:	Yellow Poplar
Economy:	Horses, poultry, hogs, apples, dairy, hay, cattle

Date Visited:

The first Kentucky Fried Chicken restaurant was established in Corbin.

"The Pelican State" — Louisiana

Capital:	Baton Rouge
Population:	4,574,836
Area (sq. mi.):	43,566
State Bird:	Brown Pelican
State Flower:	Magnolia
State Tree:	Bald Cypress
Economy:	Sugar cane, rice, cattle, soybeans, sweet potatoes

Date Visited:

The Louisiana State Capitol is the tallest capitol building in the U.S.A.

Maine   "The Pine Tree State"

Date Visited:

Capital:	Augusta
Population:	1,328,188
Area (sq. mi.):	30,865
State Bird:	Chickadee
State Flower:	White Pine Cone and Tassel
State Tree:	Eastern White Pine
Economy:	Dairy, potatoes, corn, aquaculture, cattle, maple products

Nearly 90 percent of the lobster supply of the U.S.A. is caught off the coast of Maine.

Maryland   "The Old Line State"

Date Visited:

Capital:	Annapolis
Population:	5,828,289
Area (sq. mi.):	9,775
State Bird:	Baltimore Oriole
State Flower:	Black-eyed Susan
State Tree:	White Oak
Economy:	Poultry, cattle, eggs, watermelon, tobacco, soybeans

Baseball player Babe Ruth was born in Maryland.

"The Bay State" — Massachusetts

Capital:	Boston
Population:	9,876,187
Area (sq. mi.):	7,838
State Bird:	Chickadee
State Flower:	Mayflower
State Tree:	American Elm
Economy:	Cranberries, dairy, apples, tobacco, maple products, cattle

Date Visited:

America's first subway system was built in Boston in 1897.

"The Great Lakes State" — Michigan

Capital:	Lansing
Population:	9,876,187
Area (sq. mi.):	56,809
State Bird:	Robin
State Flower:	Apple Blossom
State Tree:	White Pine
Economy:	Dairy, soybeans, hogs, grapes, apples, cherries, asparagus

Date Visited:

Michigan is the leading state in boat registrations in the U.S.A.

Minnesota   "The Gopher State"

Date Visited:

- Capital: St. Paul
- Population: 5,344,861
- Area (sq. mi.): 79,617
- State Bird: Common Loon
- State Flower: Pink & White Lady Slipper
- State Tree: Norway Pine
- Economy: Corn, hogs, soybeans, dairy, cattle, turkeys, sugar beets

The famous Mayo Clinic medical center is located in Rochester.

Mississippi   "The Magnolia State"

Date Visited:

- Capital: Jackson
- Population: 2,978,512
- Area (sq. mi.): 49,914
- State Bird: Mockingbird
- State Flower: Southern Magnolia
- State Tree: Magnolia
- Economy: Poultry, cotton, rice, cattle, sweet potatoes, pecans

The famous singer Elvis Presley was born in Tupelo on January 8, 1935.

"The Show Me State"   Missouri

Capital:	Jefferson City
Population:	6,010,688
Area (sq. mi.):	68,898
State Bird:	Bluebird
State Flower:	Hawthorn
State Tree:	Flowering Dogwood
Economy:	Soybeans, cattle, corn, rice, grapes, honey, turkeys, cotton

Date Visited:

Kansas City has more boulevards than any other city in the world, except Paris.

"The Treasure State"   Montana

Capital:	Helena
Population:	998,199
Area (sq. mi.):	145,556
State Bird:	Western Meadowlark
State Flower:	Bitterroot
State Tree:	Ponderosa Pine
Economy:	Cattle, wheat, barley, sugar beets, sheep, oats, wool

Date Visited:

Yellowstone National Park is widely held to be first national park in the world.

Nebraska   "The Cornhusker State"

Date Visited:

Capital: Lincoln
Population: 1,842,641
Area (sq. mi.): 76,878
State Bird: Western Meadowlark
State Flower: Goldenrod
State Tree: Cottonwood
Economy: Cattle, corn, soybeans, wheat, dairy, eggs, potatoes

The Reuben sandwich originated in Nebraska.

Nevada   "The Silver State"

Date Visited:

Capital: Carson City
Population: 2,723,322
Area (sq. mi.): 109,806
State Bird: Mountain Bluebird
State Flower: Sagebrush
State Tree: Bristlecone Pine
Economy: Cattle, hay, dairy, wheat, garlic, honey, hogs, barley

Nevada is the leading state in U.S. gold mining.

"The Granite State" # New Hampshire

　　　　Capital: Concord
　　Population: 1,318,194
　Area (sq. mi.): 8,969
　　　State Bird: Purple Finch
　State Flower: Purple Lilac
　　　State Tree: White Birch
　　　　Economy: Dairy, apples, cattle, corn, eggs, maple products

Date Visited:

New Hampshire established the first free public library in Peterborough in 1833.

"The Garden State" # New Jersey

　　　　Capital: Trenton
　　Population: 8,821,155
　Area (sq. mi.): 7,419
　　　State Bird: Eastern Goldfinch
　State Flower: Purple Violet
　　　State Tree: Red Oak
　　　　Economy: Horses, blueberries, dairy, cranberries asparagus

Date Visited:

New Jersey is the most densely populated state in the U.S.A.

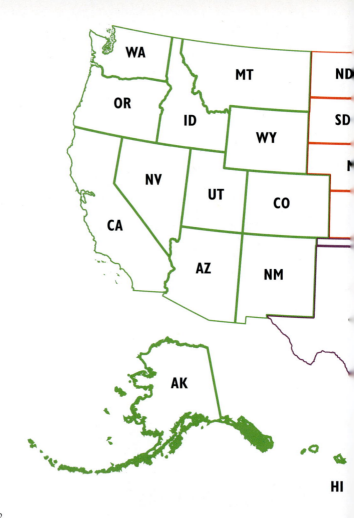

New Mexico   "The Land of Enchantment"

Date Visited:

      Capital: Santa Fe
   Population: 2,082,224
 Area (sq. mi.): 121,365
    State Bird: Roadrunner
 State Flower: Yucca
    State Tree: Piñon Pine
     Economy: Dairy, pecans, cotton, chile peppers, peanuts, onions

Santa Fe is the highest state capital in the U.S.A. at 7,000 feet.

New York   "The Empire State"

Date Visited:

      Capital: Albany
   Population: 19,465,197
 Area (sq. mi.): 47,224
    State Bird: Bluebird
 State Flower: Rose
    State Tree: Sugar Maple
     Economy: Dairy apples, hay, peas, potatoes, ducks, onions, grapes

Arthur Eldred of Troop 1 in Oceanside received the first Eagle Scout award in 1912.

"The Tar Heel State"

North Carolina

Capital:	Raleigh
Population:	9,656,401
Area (sq. mi.):	48,718
State Bird:	Cardinal
State Flower:	Flowering Dogwood
State Tree:	Pine
Economy:	Poultry, hogs, eggs, dairy, turkeys, cotton, wheat, tobacco

Date Visited:

Winston-Salem is the home of the Krispy Kreme doughnut.

"The Peace Garden State"

North Dakota

Capital:	Bismarck
Population:	683,932
Area (sq. mi.):	68,994
State Bird:	Western Meadowlark
State Flower:	Wild Prairie Rose
State Tree:	American Elm
Economy:	Wheat, cattle, sugar beets, soybeans, dry beans, sunflowers

Date Visited:

North Dakota is the leading producer of sunflowers in the U.S.A.

Ohio   "The Buckeye State"

Date Visited:

Capital:	Columbus
Population:	11,544,951
Area (sq. mi.):	40,953
State Bird:	Cardinal
State Flower:	Scarlet Carnation
State Tree:	Buckeye
Economy:	Soy beans, corn, hay, poultry, turkeys, tomatoes

Akron is the rubber capital of the world.

Oklahoma   "The Sooner State"

Date Visited:

Capital:	Oklahoma City
Population:	3,791,508
Area (sq. mi.):	68,679
State Bird:	Scissor-tailed-flycatcher
State Flower:	Mistletoe
State Tree:	Eastern Redbud
Economy:	Cattle, hogs, poultry, wheat, dairy, pecans, rye, watermelon

Famous American humorist and cowboy Will Rogers was born in Oklahoma.

"The Beaver State" — Oregon

Capital:	Salem
Population:	3,871,859
Area (sq. mi.):	96,003
State Bird:	Western Meadowlark
State Flower:	Oregon Grape
State Tree:	Douglas Fir
Economy:	Cattle, dairy, hay, hops, onions, potatoes, hazel nuts, cherries

Date Visited:

Crater Lake is the deepest lake in the U.S.A.

"The Keystone State" — Pennsylvania

Capital:	Harrisburg
Population:	12,742,886
Area (sq. mi.):	44,820
State Bird:	Ruffed Grouse
State Flower:	Mountain Laurel
State Tree:	Hemlock
Economy:	Dairy, cattle, eggs, hogs, mushrooms, poultry, potatoes

Date Visited:

Hershey is considered the chocolate capital of the U.S.A.

Rhode Island   "The Ocean State"

Date Visited:

Capital:	Providence
Population:	1,051,302
Area (sq. mi.):	1,045
State Bird:	Rhode Island Red
State Flower:	Violet
State Tree:	Red Maple
Economy:	Corn, dairy, potatoes, corn, apples, hay, honey

The International Tennis Hall of Fame is located in Newport.

South Carolina   "The Palmetto State"

Date Visited:

Capital:	Columbia
Population:	4,679,230
Area (sq. mi.):	30,111
State Bird:	Carolina Wren
State Flower:	Carolina Jessamine
State Tree:	Palmetto
Economy:	Turkeys, dairy, cattle, pecans, peanuts, watermelons

The first battle of the American Civil War took place at Fort Sumter.

"The Mount Rushmore State" — South Dakota

Capital:	Pierre
Population:	824,082
Area (sq. mi.):	30,111
State Bird:	Pheasant
State Flower:	Pasque Flower
State Tree:	White Spruce
Economy:	Cattle, corn, hogs, rye wheat, soy beans, honey

Date Visited:

The world's largest petrified wood park is located in Lemmon.

"The Volunteer State" — Tennessee

Capital:	Nashville
Population:	6,403,353
Area (sq. mi.):	41,220
State Bird:	Mockingbird
State Flower:	Iris
State Tree:	Tulip Poplar
Economy:	Cattle, poultry, wool, squash, peaches, hay, aquaculture

Date Visited:

The famous frontiersman Davy Crockett was born in Greene County.

Texas
"The Lone Star State"

Date Visited:

Capital:	Austin
Population:	25,674,681
Area (sq. mi.):	264,914
State Bird:	Mockingbird
State Flower:	Bluebonnet
State Tree:	Pecan
Economy:	Cattle, cotton, hay, rice, poultry, wheat, peanuts, pecans

The Alamo is located in San Antonio.

Utah
"The Beehive State"

Date Visited:

Capital:	Salt Lake City
Population:	2,817,222
Area (sq. mi.):	82,168
State Bird:	Seagull
State Flower:	Sego Lily
State Tree:	Blue Spruce
Economy:	Cattle, dairy, apples, cherries, peaches, pears, oats, apricots

Utah comes from the Native American Ute Tribe and means "people of the mountains."

"The Green Mountain State"   Vermont

    Capital: Montpelier
  Population: 626,431
 Area (sq. mi.): 9,249
   State Bird: Hermit Thrush
 State Flower: Red Clover
   State Tree: Sugar Maple
    Economy: Dairy, cattle, apples, maple products, eggs, honey

Date Visited:

Montpelier is the smallest state capital in the U.S.A.

"Old Dominion"   Virginia

    Capital: Richmond
  Population: 8,096,604
 Area (sq. mi.): 39,598
   State Bird: Cardinal
 State Flower: Dogwood
   State Tree: Flowering Dogwood
    Economy: Poultry, cattle, dairy, turkeys, tobacco, peanuts, corn

Date Visited:

Virginia is the home base for the U.S. Navy's Atlantic Fleet.

Washington   "The Evergreen State"

Date Visited:

Capital:	Olympia
Population:	6,830,038
Area (sq. mi.):	66,581
State Bird:	Willow Goldfinch
State Flower:	Rhododendron
State Tree:	Western Hemlock
Economy:	Apples, cherries, hops, cattle, potatoes, wheat, mint

Washington is the leading producer of apples in the world.

West Virginia   "The Mountain State"

Date Visited:

Capital:	Charleston
Population:	1,855,364
Area (sq. mi.):	24,087
State Bird:	Cardinal
State Flower:	Rhododendron
State Tree:	Sugar Maple
Economy:	Poultry, cattle, tobacco, aquaculture, honey, apples, corn

West Virginia was a part of Virginia until Virginia seceded from the Union in 1861.

"The Badger State" — Wisconsin

Capital: Madison
Population: 5,711,767
Area (sq. mi.): 54,314
State Bird: Robin
State Flower: Wood Violet
State Tree: Sugar Maple
Economy: Dairy, cattle, hogs, cranberries, apples, peas, honey

Date Visited:

Wisconsin is the dairy capital of the U.S.A.

"The Equality State" — Wyoming

Capital: Cheyenne
Population: 568,158
Area (sq. mi.): 97,105
State Bird: Meadowlark
State Flower: Indian Paintbrush
State Tree: Cottonwood
Economy: Cattle, hay, honey, sugar beets, sheep, beans, barley

Date Visited:

Wyoming was the first state to grant women the right to vote in the U.S.A.

The United States Territories

American Samoa

Guam

Northern Mariana Islands

Puerto Rico

U.S. Virgin Islands

District of Columbia

"Let God be First" — American Samoa

Capital: Pago Pago
Population: 54,719
Area (sq. mi.): 76
Economy: Coconuts, cacao, fruits, vegetables, fish, lumber

Date Visited:

The Samoan alphabet has only fourteen letters: five vowels and nine consonants.

"Where America's Day Begins" — Guam

Capital: Agana
Population: 160,378
Area (sq. mi.): 209
Economy: Fruits & vegetables, shrimp, livestock, bananas

Date Visited:

Guam was first inhabited approximately 4,000 years ago by the Chamorro people.

Northern Mariana Islands   "Land of the Valiant Lord"

Date Visited:

Capital: Saipan
Population: 51,170
Area (sq. mi.): 185
Economy: Copra, livestock, fish, fruits & vegetables

Active volcanoes exist on several islands, including Anatahan, Pagan, and Agrihan.

Puerto Rico   "All-Star Island"

Date Visited:

Capital: San Juan
Population: 3,690,923
Area (sq. mi.): 3,435
Economy: Chemicals, clothing, fruits & vegetables, fish, sugar

El Yunque is the only tropical rainforest in the U.S. National Forest System.

"American Paradise"   # U. S. Virgin Islands

    Capital: Charlotte Amalie
Population: 104,737
Area (sq. mi.): 133
   Economy: Manufacturing, fruits & vegetables, rum

Date Visited:

The United States bought the U.S. Virgin Islands from Denmark in 1917.

Washington D.C.   # District of Columbia

    Capital: Washington, D.C.
Population: 646,449
Area (sq. mi.): 68.3
   Economy: Federal Government, tourism, education, finance, public policy, scientific research

Date Visited:

D.C. is under the jurisdiction of the U.S. Congress and is not a part of any state.

Source: Brock University Map, Data & GIS Library

Canada

"From Sea to Sea"

National Capital Region: Ottawa

Population: 35,158,300

Area: 9,984,670 sq. km (3,855,103 sq. mi.)

Language: English, French

National Animal: Beaver

National Sports: Hockey & Lacrosse

National Tree: Maple

Provinces: 10

Territories: 3 (Northwest Territories, Nunavut, Yukon)

"Wild Rose Country"   Alberta

Capital:	Edmonton
Population:	3,645,257
Area (sq. km.):	640,082
Provincial Bird:	Great Horned Owl
Provincial Flower:	Wild Rose
Provincial Tree:	Lodgepole Pine
Economy:	Coal, oil, natural gas, oats, livestock, canola, barley, wheat

Date Visited:

Alberta was named after Princess Louise Caroline Alberta, daughter of Queen Victoria.

"Beautiful British Columbia"   British Columbia

Capital:	Victoria
Population:	4,400,057
Area (sq. km.):	922,509
Provincial Bird:	Steller's Jay
Provincial Flower:	Pacific Dogwood
Provincial Tree:	Western Red Cedar
Economy:	Lumber, mining, fish, fruit & vegetables

Date Visited:

British Columbia has the largest Chinese community in Canada.

Manitoba ## "Land of 100,000 Lakes"

Date Visited:

Capital:	Winnipeg
Population:	1,208,268
Area (sq. km.):	552,330
Provincial Bird:	Great Grey Owl
Provincial Flower:	Prairie Crocus
Provincial Tree:	White Spruce
Economy:	Mining, fish, wheat, dairy, livestock

Manitoba is a world leader in the production of nickel.

New Brunswick ## "The Loyalist Province"

Date Visited:

Capital:	Fredericton
Population:	751,171
Area (sq. km.):	71,377
Provincial Bird:	Blackcapped Chickadee
Provincial Flower:	Purple Violet
Provincial Tree:	Balsam Fir
Economy:	Mining, fish, shell fish (lobster & Crab), fruit, dairy, forestry

New Brunswick is Canada's only official bilingual province (English and French).

"The Rock"   Newfoundland & Labrador

Capital:	St. John's
Population:	514,536
Area (sq. km.):	370,511
Provincial Bird:	Atlantic Puffin
Provincial Flower:	Pitcher Plant
Provincial Tree:	Black Spruce
Economy:	Fish products, oil, gas, iron ore, newsprint, electricity, shell fish

Date Visited:

Norse Vikings first visited the northern tip of Newfoundland around 1000 A.D.

"Canada's Atlantic Playground"   Nova Scotia

Capital:	Halifax
Population:	921,727
Area (sq. km.):	52,939
Provincial Bird:	Osprey
Provincial Flower:	Mayflower
Provincial Tree:	Red Spruce
Economy:	Coal, fish, lobsters, lumber, pulp, paper, gypsum, blueberries

Date Visited:

Nova Scotia means "New Scotland" in Latin.

Ontario "The Heartland Province"

Date Visited:

Capital: Toronto
Population: 12,851,821
Area (sq. km.): 908,608
Provincial Bird: Common Loon
Provincial Flower: White Trillium
Provincial Tree: Eastern White Pine
Economy: Minerals, lumber, dairy, grain, manufacturing, fruits & vegetables

Toronto is Canada's financial center.

Prince Edward Island "Birthplace of Confederation"

Date Visited:

Capital: Charlottetown
Population: 140,204
Area (sq. km.): 5,686
Provincial Bird: Blue Jay
Provincial Flower: Lady Slipper
Provincial Tree: Red Oak
Economy: Potatoes, fish, fruits & vegetables (apples, onions, blueberries)

Prince Edward Island's soil is rust-colored from a high iron oxide content.

"The Beautiful Province"   Quebec

Capital:	Quebec City
Population:	7,903,001
Area (sq. km.):	1,356,547
Provincial Bird:	Snowy Owl
Provincial Flower:	Blue Flag (Iris)
Provincial Tree:	Yellow Birch
Economy:	Minerals, pulp, paper, lumber, maple syrup, dairy, fruits & vegetables

Date Visited:

French is Quebec's sole official language.

"Canada's Bread Basket"   Saskatchewan

Capital:	Regina
Population:	1,033,381
Area (sq. km.):	588,239
Provincial Bird:	Sharp-tailed Grouse
Provincial Flower:	Western Red Lilly
Provincial Tree:	White Birch
Economy:	Wheat, canola, oats, barley, flax, lentils, oil, natural gas, minerals

Date Visited:

The Athabasca Sand Dunes comprise the most northerly active sand dune formation on Earth.

Northwest Territories   "North of Sixty"

Date Visited:

Capital:	Yellow Knife
Population:	41,462
Area (sq. km.):	1,143,793
Provincial Bird:	Gyrfalcon
Provincial Flower:	Mountain Avens
Provincial Tree:	Tamarack Larch
Economy:	Oil, natural gas, fishing, diamonds, trapping (mink, wolf, lynx, fox)

The Mackenzie River is Canada's longest river (1,738 km).

Nunavut   "Our Land"

Date Visited:

Capital:	Iqaluit
Population:	31,906
Area (sq. km.):	1,877,788
Provincial Bird:	Rock Ptarmigan
Provincial Flower:	Purple Saxifrage
Economy:	Gold, diamonds, fish, Inuit arts & crafts, vegetables in green houses

Iqaluit is Canada's northernmost capital.

"Land of the Midnight Sun"   Yukon

Capital:	Whitehorse
Population:	33,897
Area (sq. km.):	474,713
Provincial Bird:	Common Raven
Provincial Flower:	Fireweed
Provincial Tree:	Subalpine Fir
Economy:	Mining gold, zinc, lead, trapping beaver, lynx, weasel, fox, mink

Date Visited:

Yukon is larger than Belgium, Denmark, Germany, and the Netherlands combined.

Ottawa   National Capital Region

Capital:	Ottawa
Population:	883,391
Area (sq. km.):	2,778
Economy:	Public Services of Canada, high-tech industries, health services and education

Date Visited:

The motto of the City of Ottawa is "Advance-Ottawa-En Avant."

Trivia Questions   U.S.A. & Canada

1. List the five regions of the U.S.A.

   _____, _____, _____, _____, _____.

2. Which state has the largest area?
   _____. And the smallest? _____.

3. Which Canadian province has the largest area?
   _____. And the smallest? _____.

4. Number of U.S. states: _____.
   Number of Canadian provinces: _____.

5. Name the five U.S. territories.

   _____, _____, _____, _____, _____.

6. Name the three Canadian territories.

   _____, _____, _____.

7. What is the U.S. national motto?

   _____.

8. What is the Canadian national motto?

   _____.

9. What is the population of the U.S.A? _____,
   What is the population of Canada? _____.

10. National tree of the U.S.A.: _____.

11. National tree of Canada: _____.

12. Languages of Canada: _____, _____.

13. Languages of the U.S.A.: _____, _____.

Trivia answers on page 60

English, French, & Spanish Top Ten Phrases

ENGLISH	FRENCH	PRONUNCIATION
Welcome	Bienvenue	bee-ehn-veh-new
Hello	Bonjour	bohn-zhoor
Please	S'il vous plaît	seel-voo-play
Thank you	Merci	mehr-see
You are welcome	De rien	duh-ryang
Good morning	Bonjour	bohn-zhoor
Good afternoon	Bonjour	bohn-zhoor
Good evening	Bonsoir	bohn-swahr
Good day	Bonjour	bohn-zhoor
Goodbye	Au revoir	oh-ruh-vwahr

ENGLISH	SPANISH	PRONUNCIATION
Welcome	Bienvenido	be-en-vay-nee-do
Hello	Hola	o-la
Please	Por favor	por-fa-vor
Thank you	Gracias	gra-syas
You are welcome	De nada	de-na-da
Good morning	Buenos días	bwe-nos-dee-as
Good afternoon	Buenas tardes	bwe-nas-tar-des
Good evening	Buenas noches	bwe-nas-no-ches
Good day	Buenos días	bwe-nos-dee-as
Goodbye	Adiós	a-dyos

Trivia Answers — U.S.A. & Canada

1. West, Midwest, Southwest, Southeast, Northeast
2. Alaska, Rhode Island
3. Quebec, Prince Edward Island
4. States: 50, Provinces: 10
5. American Samoa, Guam, Northern Marianas, Puerto Rico, U.S. Virgin Islands
6. Northwest Territories, Nunavut, Yukon
7. In God We Trust
8. From Sea to Sea
9. Population: U.S. 311,591,917   Canada 35,158,300
10. Oak
11. Maple
12. English, French
13. English, Spanish

U.S.A. License Plate Search

- 47C72N2 — Alabama
- BVN 0669 — Georgia, Clayton
- 7687 PG — Maine
- FGM774 — Alaska
- HGX 212 — Hawaii, Aloha State
- 3DD B31 — Maryland
- AAG1921 — Arizona, Grand Canyon State
- 1A VB713 — Idaho, Famous Potatoes
- 432 EY3 — Massachusetts, The Spirit of America
- 514 KZE — Arkansas, The Natural State
- G34 3404 — Illinois
- BXC 2341 — Michigan
- 6JIV337 — California
- 221 TAN — Indiana, Hamilton
- 845 CTC — Minnesota, 10,000 lakes
- 038 NAV — Colorado
- 180 RCQ — Iowa, Linn
- TAD 856 — Mississippi, Tate
- 285·XHK — Connecticut, Constitution State
- 604 ADU — Kansas, JO
- FC6 B1R — Missouri
- 731260 — Delaware, The First State
- 547 KPE — Kentucky, Fayette
- 6·09241A — Montana, Treasure State
- 981 XXH — MyFlorida.com, Sunshine State
- OIT 643 — Louisiana, Sportsman's Paradise
- 5-D2772 — Nebraska

U.S. Territories

Canadian License Plate Search

Canadian Territories

Travelers Passport U.S. Parks, U.S.A. & Canada   Credits

National Parks & Monuments

Acadia NP-heipei deutschland; Arches NP-NPS, Public Domain; Badlands NP-DrRon; Big Bend NP-eclectico63; Biscayne NP-NPS, Public Domain; Black Canyon of the Gunnison NP-Jeff Kramer; Bryce Canyon NP-Jean-christopher-BENOIST; Canyonlands NP-Phil Armitage; Capitol Reef NP-Coke Smith; Carlsbad Caverns NP-Eric Guinther; Channel Islands NP-Todd Clark; Congaree NP-jtmartin; Crater Lake NP-DrRon; Cuyahoga Valley NP-Ralph J. Davila; Death Valley NP-DrRon; Denali NP & Preserve-Nic Mcphee; Dry Tortogas NP-NPS, Public Domain; Everglades NP-NPS, Public Domain; Gates of the Arctic NP-U.S. Fish & Wildlife,PD; Glacier Bay NP-Randy Roach; Glacier NP-Dave Grickson, USF&WS, PD; Grand Canyon NP-Luca Galuzzi; Grand Teton NP-Jon Sullivan; Great Basin NP-NPS, Public Domain; Great Sand Dunes NP & Preserve-Phil Armitage; Great Smoky NP-Uschick; Guadalupe NP-Joyradose; Haleakala NP-DrRon; Hawaii Volcanoes NP-USGS PD; Hot Springs NP-Chris Light; Isle Royale NP-Bob Walker; Joshua Tree NP-DrRon ; Katimal NP and Preserve-NOAA PD; Kenai Fjords NP-Balaz Bamucs; Kings Canyon NP-Victor Gane; Kobuk Valley NP-Anthony Remboldt; Lake Clark NP-NPS, Public Domain; Lassen Volcanic NP-Av9; Mammoth Cave NP-Navin 75; Mesa Verde NP-Andreas F. Borchert;

Mount Rainer NP-Stan Sherbs; NP of American Samoa-Peter Craig, NPS, PD; North Cascades NP-Walter Siegmund; Olympic NP-DrRon; Petrified Forest NP-finetooth; Pinnacles NP-Brucken Inaglory; Redwood NP-Michael Schweepe; Rocky Mountain NP-DrRon; Saguaro NP-Saguaro pictures; Sequoia NP-Tuxyso; Shenandoah NP-DrRon; Theodore Roosevelt NP-NPS, PD; Virgin Island NP-Ben Whitney; Voyageurs NP-Ed Lombard, NPS, PD; Wind Cave NP-Dave Bunnell; Wrangell-St. Elias NP & Preserve-R McGimsey, USGS, PD; Yellowstone NP-Mike Burk; Yosemite NP-Mike Burk; Zion NP-Coke Smith; Cabrillo NM-DrRon; Castle Clinton NM-Jim Henderson PD; Golden Gate Rec Area-DrRon; Jefferson Nat'l Expansion Monument-Bev Sykes; Mt. Rushmore NM-DrRon; Mt. St. Helen's National Volcanic Monument-Lyn Topinka, USGS, PD; Oregon Caves NM & Preserve-David Monniaux; Statue of Liberty NM-Mike Burk; WWII Valor in Pacific NM-Mike Burk.

Welcome Signs U.S.A.
AK: Richard Martin; OR: Oregon Department Transportation; Other 48 States: Dr. Ron Snipe.

Welcome Signs Canada
Alberta: Raymond Hitchcock; British Columbia: Hans-Peter Eckhardt; Manitoba: Government of Manitoba; New Brunswick: Dr Ron Snipe; Newfoundland: Government of Newfoundland; NW Territories: Government Tourist Office; Nova Scotia: Dennis Jarvis; Nunavut: Government of Nunavut; Ontario: Dr. Ron Snipe; Prince Edward Island: Government of P.E.I.; Quebec: Dr. Ron Snipe; Saskatchewan: Tdot778; Yukon: ZOOP; National Capital Region: public domain.

U.S.A. Capitals
All 50 photos: Dr. Ron Snipe, 2005-2013.

U.S.A. Territories
American Samoa: (l) Thomas Marki, (r) miles530 of NOAA; Guam: (l) USAF-A.M. Lawrence, (r) Abasaa; Northern Marianas: Abasaa; Puerto Rico: Dr. Ron Snipe; U.S. Virgin Islands: (l) Johnpaulribaudo, (r) smallbones.

Canadian Government Buildings
Alberta: Zeitlupe; British Columbia: Dr. Ron Snipe; Manitoba: Canuks4ever83; New Brunswick: Benson Kua; Newfoundland: David P. Janes; Northwest Territories: wintercity296; Nova Scotia: Louperivois; Nunavut: Ansgar Walk; Ontario: Benson Kua; Prince Edward Island: Share Bear; Quebec: Christopher Finot; Saskatchewan: M Readey; Yukon: OwnWork

U.S.A. License Plates
All photos public domain.

U.S.A. Territories License Plates
American Samoa: monroedictator; Guam, Northern Mariana Islands, Puerto Rico, U.S. Virgin Islands: Jerry Woody.

Canadian License Plates
Alberta, British Columbia, Manitoba, NW Territories, Saskatchewan: Jerry Woody; Ontario, Prince Edward Island: Dickelbers; New Brunswick: Campbell Showing; Newfoundland: Ramses31; Nova Scotia: Government of Nova Scotia; Nunavut: Government of Nunavut; Quebec: Lionel Bartel; Yukon: RobinsonCrusoe.

National Capital Buildings
U.S.A. Capitol Buildings: pg. 16-Martin Falbisoner; pg. 47-Architect of the Capitol. Canadian Parliament: pg. 15-Steven W. Dengler; pg. 57-Public Domain.

Maps, U.S.A. and Canada
U.S.A. Outline Map: Public Domain; Canada Outline Map: Brock University Map, Data & GIS Library

Author: Ron Snipe, Ph.D

Managing Editor: Elizabeth Snipe

Designer: Zachary Snipe, Esq.

Copy Editor: Victoria Snipe

Consultant: Vickie Grieve

Typography & Print Production:
Mike Burk Production Services
www.mikeburk.com